Grade **1.1**

Scott Foresman
Practice Book

PEARSON
Scott Foresman

Editorial Offices: Glenview, Illinois • Parsippany, New Jersey • New York, New York
Sales Offices: Needham, Massachusetts • Duluth, Georgia • Glenview, Illinois
Coppell, Texas • Sacramento, California • Mesa, Arizona

ISBN: 0-328-14515-7

24 25 26 27 V011 17 16 15 14 13

Contents

Unit 1
Animals, Tame and Wild

Contents

Unit 2
Communities

Practice Book

Family Times

You are your child's first and best teacher!

This week we're

Reading Sam, Come Back!

Talking About How people take care of their pets

Learning About Short *a*
Final *ck*
Character

Here are ways to help your child practice skills while having fun!

Day 1

Write these words on a sheet of paper: *man, men, can, had, lad, run, ran, cat, cot, bat.* Read each word aloud. Have your child tell you if the word has the short *a* sound. If it does, have your child write it and read it aloud.

Day 2

Write these words on a sheet of paper: *back, sack, pack, rack, tack.* Have your child read the words. Then have him or her act out the word as you guess it.

Day 3

Copy these words onto cards: *on, way,* and *in.* Tell your child these are "Boing" words. Read a story together. If a "Boing" word is read, your child should jump up and yell, "Boing!"

Day 4

Write each spelling word on a card: *at, can, cat, back, dad, am, bat, mad, ran, sack.* Have your child sort the words according to his or her own rules. Then, have him or her spell each word.

Day 5

This week your child is learning about the characters in a story. Read a story to your child. Have your child tell you who the story is about.

Oh, That Fat Cat!

Materials crayons

Game Directions

1. Together, read the words in each space.
2. Choose a crayon and pick one of the paths. Color in the Start box.
3. Flip a coin. If the coin lands heads up, read aloud the word in the next box, and then color it in. If the coin lands tails up, play passes to the other player. The first player to color in the End box wins!

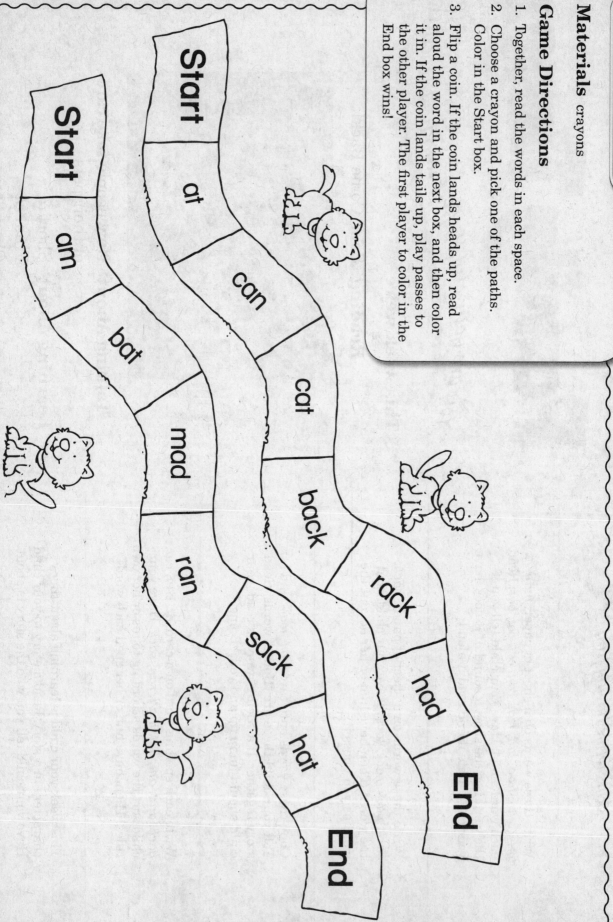

Start — at — can — cat — back — rack — had — **End**

Start — bat — mad — ran — sack — hat — **End**

Start — am

Name _____

Say the word for each picture.
Write a on the line if you hear the **short a** sound.

c<u>a</u>t

1.
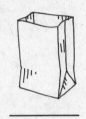
_____
- - - - - - -
b _____ g

2.

_____
- - - - - - -
f _____ n

3.

_____
- - - - - - -
m _____ p

4.

_____
- - - - - - -
m _____ p

5.

_____
- - - - - - -
c _____ n

6.

_____
- - - - - - -
m _____ n

7.

_____
- - - - - - -
p _____ g

8.

_____
- - - - - - -
v _____ n

Find the picture whose name has the **short a** sound.
Mark the ⬭ to show your answer.

9. ⬭   ⬭   ⬭

10. ⬭   ⬭   ⬭

School + Home

Home Activity Your child has reviewed words with the short *a* sound heard in *cat*. Work with your child to make words that rhyme with *cat* and *man*.

© Pearson Education 1

Name _____

Look at the pictures.

Sam   **Nan**   **Max**

Circle the picture that shows what the animal likes.

I. Nan

2. Max   

3. Sam   

Fill in the ⬭ .

4. Sam is a

⬭ **bat**   ⬭ **rat**   ⬭ **cat**

Draw a character from the story you have read.

5.

Home Activity Your child learned about characters in stories. As you read stories with your child, point out details that tell what the character enjoys and what it looks like.

4 **Comprehension** Character   **Practice Book Unit 1**

Name _____

Say the word for each picture.
Write ck on the line if the word has the same ending sound as .

1.

ta _____

2.

ba _____

3.

fa _____

4.
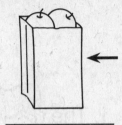
sa _____

5.
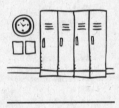
ha _____

6.

ja _____

7.

pa _____

8.

ca _____

Find the word that has the same ending sound as .
Mark the ⬭ to show your answer.

9. ⬭ tap
   ⬭ tan
   ⬭ tack

10. ⬭ rack
    ⬭ rag
    ⬭ ram

© Pearson Education 1

Home Activity Your child practiced reading words that end in *ck*. Help your child write words that rhyme with *sack*.

Name _____

Pick a word from the box to finish each sentence.
Write it on the line.

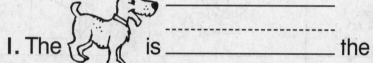

| in | on | way |

1. The _____ is _____ the  .

2. We go that _____ to the  .

3. The _____ is _____ the  .

Draw the puppy on the mat.

4.

© Pearson Education 1

Home Activity This week your child learned to read the words *in, on,* and *way*. Write each word on a card. Have your child read each word and then use it in a sentence.

Name _____

Pick a word to finish each sentence.
Write it on the line.

| in on way |

1. The cat is _____ the bag.

2. The bat is _____ the hat.

3. That is the _____ to the .

Draw the way to the .

4.

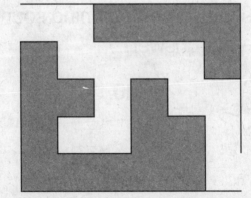

School + Home

Home Activity This week your child learned to read the words *in, on,* and *way.* Write each word on a card. Place an object in or on items in your home. Have your child point to the *in* or *on* card that describes the object's location. Then have your child pick up the *way* card while saying, "We go this *way.*"

Name _____

<u>b</u>ag <u>c</u>an <u>f</u>ox <u>j</u>ack <u>m</u>ap <u>P</u>at <u>t</u>ack <u>w</u>ax

Pick a letter from the box to begin each word.
Write it on the line.

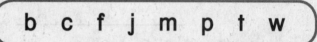
b c f j m p t w

1.
_____ at

2.
_____ an

3.
_____ ap

4.
_____ an

5.
_____ ag

6.
_____ am

7.
_____ an

8.
_____ ag

Find the word that has the same beginning sound as the picture.
Mark the ⬭ to show your answer.

9. ⬭ lad
   ⬭ dad
   ⬭ had

10. ⬭ hat
    ⬭ rat
    ⬭ sat

 Home Activity Your child reviewed words that begin with the letters *b, c, f, h, j, m, p, r, t,* and *w.* Help your child make a list of foods that begin with these letters.

© Pearson Education 1

Name _____

ma**d**　　wa**g**　　ja**m**　　pa**n**　　ca**p**　　bu**s**　　ma**t**

Pick a letter from the box
to finish each word.
Write it on the line.

d　g　m　n　p　s　t

1.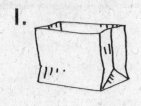
ba ____

2.
ca ____

3.
da ____

4.
ga ____

5.
ha ____

6.
ma ____

7.
ha ____

8.
va ____

Find the word that has the same ending sound as the picture.
Mark the ⬭ to show your answer.

9. ⬭ cap
　 ⬭ tag
　 ⬭ tan

10. ⬭ sag
　　⬭ sad
　　⬭ sat

Home Activity Your child reviewed words that end with the letters *d, g, m, n, p, s,* and *t.* Have your child say a word that rhymes with each word they finished in the exercise above.

Practice Book Unit 1　　　**Phonics** Final Consonants Review　**9**

Name _____

Circle the cover.

Place an X over the book about bats.

Circle the book that Dan wrote.
Draw a box around the book Max wrote.

© Pearson Education 1

Home Activity Your child learned to use the title and picture on a book cover to figure out what the book is about. Your child also learned to look for more information on the title page of the book. Point out the cover and title page of the next book you read together.

Family Times

Name

You are your child's first and best teacher!

This week we're

Reading Pig in a Wig

Talking About How people can help animals

Learning About Short *i*
Final *x*
Realism and Fantasy

Here are ways to help your child practice skills while having fun!

Day 1

Say a short *i* word, and ask your child to say a rhyming word. Write both words. Continue until you have ten words. Then have him or her read the list. Some words you might use are *fix, fig, kid, rip,* and *win.*

Day 2

Write each word on a card: *tax, wax, six, mix, fix.* Ask your child to read the words and make up sentences for each word.

Day 3

Write these words: *and, take, up.* Have your child read them. Then have him or her practice "printing" the words using their index finger on a table. Next, have your child write the words on paper and read them.

Day 4

Together, write a funny set of directions for what to do with a wig. Use this week's spelling words: *in, it, did, sit, six, fix, lip, mix, pin, wig.*

Day 5

This week your child is learning the difference between what could really happen and what could not really happen in a story. As you read books with your child, discuss whether the people or animals in the story do things that real people or animals do.

Roll a Word

Materials scissors, crayons or markers, white and colored paper

Game Directions

1. Cut a colored piece of paper into eight pieces and copy one of the letters below onto each piece. Place all of the pieces face down.

2. Cut a white piece of paper into eight pieces and copy one of the word parts shown below onto each piece.

3. Each player picks four white pieces and one colored piece. Use the pieces to make as many real words as possible.

b	d	f	w
p	s	h	l

ig	it	in	ill
im	id	ip	ix

Name _____

Say the word for each picture.
Write i on the line if you hear the **short i** sound.

p<u>i</u>g

1.

k _____ ck

2.

h _____ t

3.

t _____ ck

4.

f _____ n

5.

p _____ n

6.

d _____ g

7.

w _____ g

8.

z _____ p

Find the word that has the same middle sound as .
Mark the ⬭ to show your answer.

9. ⬭ hat
⬭ hid
⬭ ham

10. ⬭ tap
⬭ pal
⬭ tip

 School + Home **Home Activity** Your child reviewed words with the short *i* sound heard in *pig*. Help your child make up fun rhymes using short *i* words, such as *The big pig in the wig can dig and do a jig.*

Name _____

Look at each pair of pictures.
Circle the picture that shows something that could not
really happen.

1.

2.

3.

4.

Draw a picture of something that could not really happen.

5.

Home Activity Your child learned about the difference between what could really happen and what is make-believe. As you read stories with your child, have your child tell you whether the story could or could not really happen.

14 **Comprehension** Realism and Fantasy

Name _____

Say the word for each picture.
Write x on the line if the word has the same ending sound as **ax**.

ax

I.	2. 	3. 	4.
si ____	wa ____	li ____	ki ____

5. 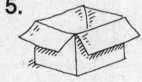	6.	7.	8. 
bo ____	mi ____	si ____	fi ____

Find the word that has the same ending sound as **6** .
Mark the ⬭ to show your answer.

9. ⬭ tax
   ⬭ tan
   ⬭ tip

10. ⬭ at
    ⬭ am
    ⬭ ax

© Pearson Education 1

Home Activity Your child practiced reading words that end with *x*. Write *six, mix,* and *fix* on cards. Have your child choose a card, read the word, and use it in a sentence.

Name _____

Pick a word from the box to finish each sentence.
Write it on the line.

| and | take | up |

1. I have a cat _____ five  .

2. One is _____ on Sam.

3. You can _____ two.

Draw the cat and two   .

4.

Draw a up on you.

5.

Home Activity This week your child learned to read the words *and, take,* and *up.* As you read with your child, encourage him or her to point out these words in print.

© Pearson Education 1

Name _____

Pick a word to finish each sentence.
Write it on the line.

> and   play   take   up

_____
- - - - - - - - - - - - - - - - - -
1. We _____ .

_____
- - - - - - - - - - - - - - - - - -
2. Look at you _____ me.

_____
- - - - - - - - - - - - - - - - - -
3. We go _____ .

_____
- - - - - - - - - - - - - - - - - -
4. You can _____ this.

Draw two friends at play.

5.

Home Activity This week your child learned to read the words *and, play, take,* and *up.* Help your child make up a story that uses these words. Write the story as your child tells it. Then invite him or her to draw a picture that goes with the story.

© Pearson Education 1

Name _____

Read the word.
Circle the picture for each word.

can

1. tack

2. pan

3. map

4. sack

5. fan

6. hat

7. sax  **6**

8. back

Find the word that has the same middle sound as .
Mark the ⬭ to show your answer.

9. ⬭ sag
   ⬭ sip
   ⬭ six

10. ⬭ bit
    ⬭ bat
    ⬭ bin

© Pearson Education 1

Home Activity Your child reviewed words with the short *a* sound. Go on a "short *a* hunt" around your home with your child. Together, make a list of things you find whose names have a short *a* sound.

Practice Book Unit 1

Name _____

Circle the word for each picture.

pa**ck**

1. 	rack rat	2. 	sad sack
3. 	kit kick	4.	bag back
5. 	pick pig	6. 	sip sick
7. 	lick lid	8.	tack tab

Find the word that has the same ending sound as  .
Mark the ⬭ to show your answer.

9. ⬭ rap
⬭ rack
⬭ ram

10. ⬭ tick
⬭ tin
⬭ tip

 School + Home **Home Activity** Your child reviewed words that end with *ck*. Help your child write words that end in *ck*. Together, use them to make up nonsense rhymes. (For example, *Put your backpack in a sack on the rack.*)

© Pearson Education 1

Name _____

1. **Circle** the shelf with encyclopedias and dictionaries.

2. **Draw** a box around the shelf with books about real things.

3. **Place** an X over the computer.

4. **Underline** the shelves of books on tape.

5. **Draw** an arrow to the shelf with videos and DVDs.

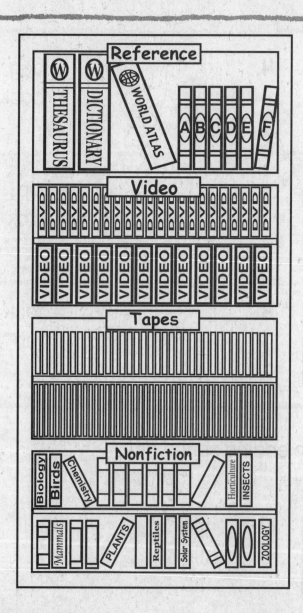

© Pearson Education 1

Home Activity Your child learned to find resources in the library. Visit your local library with your child and help him or her find the nonfiction picture books, encyclopedias, dictionaries, books on tape, videos, and the library's computers.

20 **Research and Study Skills** Media Center

Family Times

How can this
big blue ox help?

The Big Blue Ox

by Susan Stevens Crummel
illustrated by Jamal Simons

You are your child's first and best teacher!

This week we're

Reading The Big Blue Ox

Talking About How animals can help people

Learning About Short *o*
-s Plurals
Character and Setting

1

---

*Here are ways to help your child practice
skills while having fun!*

Day 1

Write these words on paper: *rock, lock, hop, mop, top, got, hot, pot.* Then using crayons, write the first letter of each word in one color and have your child finish writing the word in another color and read the words.

Day 2

Together, write silly rhymes using the plural forms of the words in this list: *cat, rat, pig, wig, sack, tack, mop, top, rock, sock.*

Day 3

Write the following codes on a sheet of paper: 1 = e, 2 = g, 3 = h, 4 = k, 5 = l, 6 = p, 7 = s, 8 = t, 9 = u. Then write the following secret codes: 2-1-8, 3-1-5-6, 9-7-1. Have your child solve the code by writing the letters to each word and reading the words. (*get, help, use*)

Day 4

Read each spelling word aloud: *mom, hot, hop, pot, pop, ox, lock, mop, got, rock.* Have your child write the words as you read them and then write the plural forms of *pot, lock,* and *rock.*

Day 5

This week your child is learning about the characters and setting in a story. Read a story to your child. Have your child tell you who the story is about and name any other people or animals in the story. Ask your child to tell you where the story takes place.

4

Hop, Hop Frog

Materials index cards, marker, paper, pencil, 1 coin per player

Game Directions

1. Copy the words below on index cards and place the cards face down on the table.

2. Each player puts a coin on Start. The first player picks a word card and reads it aloud. Then he or she writes the plural form of the word on paper.

3. Each time a player writes the plural form of the word correctly, he or she can "hop" his or her coin to the next lily pad. Play then continues to the next player.

cob	job	rod
mob	cot	dot
pot	top	mop
dock	lock	lot
rock	sock	pod

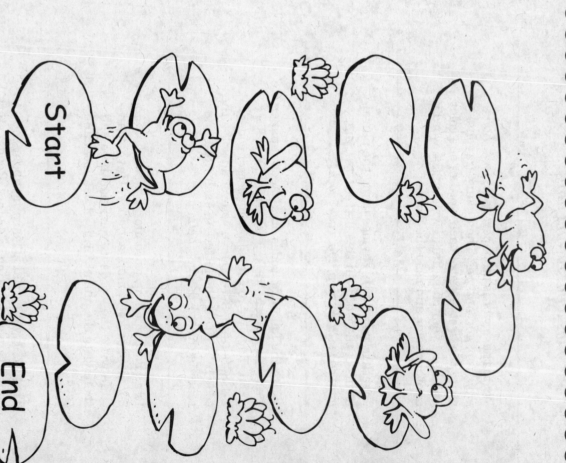

Start

End

Name _____

Say the word for each picture.
Circle the picture if the word has
the **short o** sound you hear in **top**.

t<u>o</u>p

1.

2.

3.

4.

5.

6.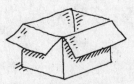

7.

8.

9.

10.

11.

12.

13.

14.

15.

© Pearson Education 1

Home Activity Your child identified words that contain the short *o* sound heard in *top*. Encourage your child to use the short *o* words pictured above in sentences.

Name _____

Look at each pair of pictures.
Circle the pictures that show characters in settings that make sense.

1.

2.

3.

4.

Draw a picture of an animal from a story you have read.
Show where it lives.

5.

© Pearson Education 1

Home Activity Your child learned about characters and places in a story. As you read together, have your child tell you what he or she knows about the characters and settings in the stories.

Name _____

Circle a word to match each picture.

pan<u>s</u>

1. 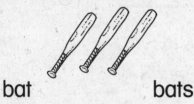 bat bats	**2.** mop mops
3.  rock rocks	**4.** pig pigs
5.  top tops	**6.**  cap caps
7. kit kits	**8.**  sack sacks

Draw a picture for each word.

9. cats

10. fox

© Pearson Education 1

School + Home

Home Activity Your child identified singular and plural nouns. Have your child name items around the house. Point out the use of *-s* at the end of many plural words, such as *books, apples,* and *bowls.*

Name _____

Pick a word from the box to finish each sentence.
Write it on the line.

get   help   use

1. Can I _____ your  ?

2. My dogs _____ you go.

3. You can _____ there fast!

Draw an animal that helps.

4.

Draw a picture of something you use to help with your schoolwork.

5.

© Pearson Education 1

Home Activity This week your child learned to read the words *get, help,* and *use.* Encourage your child to find these words in everyday print, such as on signs.

26 **High-Frequency Words**   **Practice Book Unit 1**

Name _____

Pick a word from the box to finish each sentence.
Write it on the line.

get   help   mud   town   use

1. Max and I are in the _____ .

2. We can _____ that!

3. They _____ Max and me.

4. We _____ up.

5. We go to the _____ .

Home Activity This week your child learned to read the words *get, help, mud, town,* and *use.* Help your child make up a silly story that uses these words. Write the story as your child tells it. Then invite him or her to draw a picture to go with the story.

© Pearson Education 1

Name _____

Read the word.
Circle the picture for each word.

bib

---

1. lid →

2. dig

---

3. wig

4. pin

---

5. pig

6. rip

---

7. kick

8. fin

Find the picture whose name has the **short *i*** sound.
Mark the ⬭ to show your answer.

9. ⬭ ⬭ ⬭

10. ⬭ ⬭ ⬭

Home Activity Your child practiced reading words with the short *i* sound heard in *bib*. Work with your child to write words that rhyme with *tin* and *big*.

© Pearson Education 1

Name _____

Read the word.
Circle the word for each picture.

o**x**

| 1. **6** | six <br> sits | 2.  | wag <br> wax |

| 3.  | fog <br> fox | 4. | mix <br> mitt |

| 5. | sax <br> sack | 6. | box <br> bat |

| 7.  | sick <br> six | 8.  | fix <br> fin |

Find the word that has the same ending sound as **6** .
Mark the ⬭ to show your answer.

9. ⬭ tax
   ⬭ tan
   ⬭ tick

10. ⬭ it
    ⬭ am
    ⬭ ax

© Pearson Education 1

School + Home

Home Activity Your child practiced reading words that end with *x*. Write *six, mix,* and *fix* on cards. Have your child draw a card, read the word, and give clues to its meaning for you to guess.

Practice Book Unit 1   **Phonics** Final *x* Review   **29**

Name _____

1. **Circle** the man who works on the farm.

2. **Make** a box around the cow.

3. **Put** an X on the barn.

4. **Write** the word that names the animal the farmer is feeding.

    _____

    - - - - - - - - - - - - - - - - -

    _____

5. **Write** the word that names the animal in the mud.

    _____

    - - - - - - - - - - - - - - - - -

    _____

Home Activity Your child learned about words in a picture dictionary. Find a picture dictionary at the library and help your child use it to understand the meanings of related words.

30 **Research and Study Skills** Picture Dictionary   **Practice Book Unit 1**

Family Times

Name _____

You are your child's first and best teacher!

This week we're

Reading A Fox and a Kit

How does a mother fox take care of her kit?

A Fox and a Kit
by Lupe Romero
Illustrated by Charles Lehman

Talking About What we can learn about animals by watching them

Learning About Inflected Ending -s
Inflected Ending -ing
Main Idea

Here are ways to help your child practice skills while having fun!

Day 1
Write each of the following words on an index card: *nap, sit, win, fit, hit*. Write *s* on another card. Have your child read a word to you. Place the *s* on the end of the word. Have your child read the new word.

Day 2
Write each of the following words on an index card: *they, I, she, he, we, is, are, the, fox, cat, play, plays, playing, eat, eats, eating*. Take turns making sentences using as many of the words as possible.

Day 3
Write these words and have your child read them: *eat, her, this, too*. Then cut index cards into nine pieces. Write a letter on each piece: *a, e, h, i, o, o, r, s, t*. Have your child duplicate each word using the letters.

Day 4
Give your child this list of spelling words: *nap, naps, sit, sits, win, wins, fit, fits, hit, hits*. Make up a sentence for one word, but say "beep" for the spelling word. Have your child identify the word for the "beep" space and then spell it.

Day 5
This week your child is learning about the main idea in a story. As you read stories with your child, discuss with him or her what the story was mainly about.

Materials marker, index cards

Game Directions

1. Write each word onto an index card and place the cards face down on the table.

2. The first player chooses one card and reads it in the sentence "I ____." (Example: "I kick.")

3. Then the player points to another player and says "She (or He) ____." and names the same action, adding -s. (Example: "She kicks.")

4. Finally, both players say "We are ____." and name the action, adding -ing to the end of the word. (Example: "We are kicking.") Play continues with the second player choosing a card.

kick	play
help	rock
see	look
pick	eat
pack	lock

Name _____

Add -s to each word.
Write the new word on the line.

1. hop _____   2. sit _____

3. see _____ | 4. pat _____ | 5. help _____

Use the words you wrote to finish the sentences.
Write the words on the lines.

6. Jack _____ a big dog.

7. Jack _____ the dog.

8. Jack _____ on a rock.

9. The dog _____ Jack.

10. The dog _____ on Jack.

 Home Activity Your child added -s to verbs. Have your child write the verbs *see, fan, nap, dig, sit, hop, jog,* and *mop,* and add an -s to each verb. Have your child pick a verb and use it in a sentence about you, such as *Mommy hops.* Then act out the sentence.

Name _____

Read the story.
Circle the sentence that tells best what the story is about.
Draw a picture that shows what the story is about.

_____

1. Dan has a cat.   2.

   The cat is tan.

   The cat is fat.

   Dan has a fat, tan cat.

_____

3. Liz is a fox.   4.

   Liz has a kit.

   Liz likes to play.

   The kit likes to play.

   Liz and her kit like to play.

_____

Write the name of a story you have read.
Draw a picture that shows what the story is about.

_____

5. _____

Home Activity Your child learned about the main idea of a story. As you read stories together, have your child tell you the main idea.

Name _____

Add -ing to each word.
Write the new word on the line.

1. help _____   2. look _____

3. fix _____ | 4. lick _____ | 5. play _____

Use the words you wrote to finish the sentences.
Write the words on the lines.

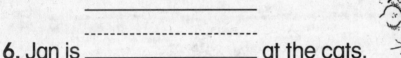

6. Jan is _____ at the cats.

7. Jan is _____ the cats.

8. The cats are _____ with the can.

9. The big cat is _____ the little cat.

10. Jan is _____ the lock.

Home Activity Your child added -ing to verbs. Have your child write the verbs *lick, rock, kick, eat,* and *mix* on slips of paper. Then have your child add -ing to each verb. Have your child pick a slip of paper and act out the word for you to guess.

Name _____

Pick a word from the box to finish each sentence.
Write it on the line.
Remember to begin a sentence with a capital letter.

eat	her	this	too

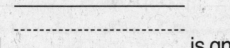

_____

1. _____ is an _____ .

_____

2. The _____ likes to _____ .

_____

3. Can we help _____ ?

_____

4. She has a black dog _____ .

Draw an animal eating with its baby.

5.

© Pearson Education 1

Home Activity This week your child learned to read the words *eat, her, this,* and *too.* Look through books to find these words in print and have your child read them aloud.

Name _____

Circle a word to finish each sentence.
Write it on the line.

animals   dinner
_____
- -

1. We see the _____ .

This   Her
_____
- -

2. _____ is a big cat.

---

this   too
_____
- -

3. That is a big cat _____ .

---

watch   dinner
_____
- -

4. The cats eat _____ .

---

her   we
_____
- -

5. The big one is _____ mom.

---

dinner   eat
_____
- -

6. We watch the _____ too.

School + Home   **Home Activity** This week your child learned to read the words *animals, dinner, eat, her, this, too,* and *watch.* Help your child use as many of these words as possible to make up a story about a day spent with friendly animals. Write the story as your child tells it. Invite him or her to draw a picture of the story.

© Pearson Education 1

Name _____

Say the word for each picture.
Write o on the line if you hear the **short o** sound.

 p<u>o</u>t

1.  f ___ x

2.  h ___ t

3. s ___ ck

4.  c ___ t

5.  b ___ x

6.  b ___ t

7. t ___ p

8. l ___ ck

Find the word that has the same middle sound as .
Mark the ⬭ to show your answer.

9. ⬭ jam
   ⬭ job
   ⬭ jig

10. ⬭ not
    ⬭ nag
    ⬭ nick

 Home Activity Your child reviewed words with the short o sound heard in *hot*. Work with your child to make words that rhyme with *hot* or *lock*.

Name _____

Say the word for each picture.
Write -s if the picture shows more than one.

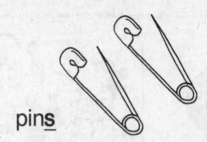

pin<u>s</u>

I.

bat _____

2.

cat _____

3.

kid _____

4.

pig _____

5.

can _____

6.

rat _____

7.

sock _____

8.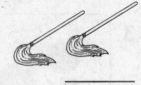

mop _____

Find the word that means more than one.
Mark the ⬯ to show your answer.

9. ⬯ gas
   ⬯ hats
   ⬯ is

10. ⬯ this
    ⬯ was
    ⬯ pots

 Home Activity Your child reviewed nouns that mean more than one. Have your child make up a sentence about each animal grouping on this page.

Name _____

Look at the signs and pictures.
Draw a line from each sign to the picture it fits.

1.

2.

3.

Draw a sign to tell people to keep off the grass.

Home Activity Your child learned to read symbols on signs to get information. As you run errands with your child this week, point out the signs and symbols you pass and discuss their meanings.

40 **Research and Study Skills** Signs

Practice Book Unit 1

© Pearson Education 1

Family Times

Name

You are your child's first and best teacher!

This week we're

Reading Get the Egg!

Get the Egg!

Can Brad and Kim help save the red bird's egg?

Talking About Wild animals we can find in our own backyards

Learning About Short *e*
Initial Blends
Realism and Fantasy

Here are ways to help your child practice skills while having fun!

Day 1

Write each word on an index card: *pat, pot, pet, pig, peg, beg, bag, big, men, man, set, sat, sit.* Have your child read each word aloud. When the child correctly identifies a short *e* word, together stand up and twirl around or do another fun action.

Day 2

Give your child this list of words: *step, stop, skip, sled, slip, spot, flat, swim, glad, drip, flip, plan, clip.* Then face away. Have your child use his or her finger to "write" each word in large letters on your back. You guess the word.

Day 3

Write the following words in a list on lined paper: *saw, small, tree, your.* Look for each word in a magazine. Have your child circle the words.

Day 4

Write the following spelling words on cards: *bed, men, red, step, ten, net, leg, jet, sled, wet.* Have your child sort the words into groups of their choosing.

Day 5

This week your child is learning the difference between what could really happen and what could not really happen in a story. As you read together, discuss whether the events could really happen.

Seek and Say

Materials markers, index cards

Game Directions

1. Copy the words on page 3 onto index cards. Pick a room or rooms in the house where you and your child can play. Place as many cards as possible on or under objects with a short *e* sound in the name such as the *leg* of a table, a *peg* on the wall, a *desk*, a *bed*, a *bell*, or even a *pet bed*. Place the rest anywhere they might be found.

2. Each player should enter the room and start looking for cards. When a player finds a card, he or she should say, "Found one!" All players stop looking while that player names the item the card was found on or under and says whether or not that object has a short *e* in the name.

3. Then the player reads aloud the word on the card and shows it to the other players.

4. Play continues with all players looking for cards until all cards are found.

net	jet	pet
wet	beg	leg
peg	hen	men
pen	ten	get
let	met	den

Name _____

Circle the word for each picture.

web

1.

mitt   men   man

2.

bed   bid   bad

3.

pen   pan   pin

4. **10**

tin   tan   ten

5.

pet   pot   pat

6.

net   not   nip

7.

log   lag   leg

8.

jam   jet   jog

9.

hat   hen   hit

10.

pot   pit   pet

© Pearson Education 1

 School + Home

Home Activity Your child practiced reading words with the short *e* sound heard in *web*. Work with your child to make words that rhyme with *pet* or *bell*.

Name _____

Look at each pair of pictures.
Circle the picture that shows something that could really happen.

1.

2.

3.

4.

Draw a picture of something that could not happen in real life.

5.

© Pearson Education 1

Home Activity Your child learned about the difference between what could really happen and what is make-believe. As you read stories with your child, have your child tell you whether the story could really happen.

44 **Comprehension** Realism and Fantasy   **Practice Book Unit 1**

Name _____

Pick letters from the box to finish each word.
Write the letters on the line.

 <u>sw</u>im

bl cl cr dr fl fr gr sl sm st

1. _____ ag

2. _____ ock

3. _____ ap

4. _____ ess

5. _____ ab

6. _____ og

7. _____ ell

8. _____ ed

9. _____ ep

10. _____ in

© Pearson Education 1

 School + Home **Home Activity** Your child identified words with initial blends (*flag, dress, sled*). Help your child make up silly sentences that each contain words beginning with just one blend, such as *Freddy frog likes French fries*.

Name _____

Pick a word from the box to finish each sentence.
Write it on the line. **Remember** to use a capital letter at the beginning of a sentence.

saw   small   tree   your

_____
- - - - - - - - - - - - - - - - - - -
1. We _____ a tree.

_____
- - - - - - - - - - - - - - - - - - -
2. It was not a big _____.

_____
- - - - - - - - - - - - - - - - - - -
3. Do you like this _____ tree?

_____
- - - - - - - - - - - - - - - - - - -
4. _____ tree is not wet.

Draw two small trees.

5.

Home Activity This week your child learned to read the words *saw, small, tree,* and *your*. Make flashcards with one word on each card. Mix them up and have your child read the words.

© Pearson Education 1

Name _____

Pick a word from the box to finish each sentence.
Write it on the line.

> nest   saw   small   tree   your

_____
I. We _____ a bird.

_____
2. The bird was not _____.

_____
3. We saw it go to a _____.

_____
4. The bird sat in its _____.

_____
5. We can use _____.

Home Activity This week your child learned to read the words *bird, nest, saw, small, tree,* and *your.* Write these words on cards. Take turns drawing two cards. Try to use both words in one sentence. Help your child write the sentences.

Use the word in ( ) to finish each sentence.
Write it on the line.
Add -s if needed.

Mom **sits**.
Mick and Bess **swim**.

(hop)

_____

I. Bess _____ up the hill.

(dig)

_____

----

2. She _____ .

(play)

_____

----

3. Mom and Mick _____ with her.

(get)

_____

----

4. Mick _____ wet.

Find the sentence that tells about the picture.
Mark the ⬭ to show your answer.

5. ⬭ Moms sees Bess and Mick.
   ⬭ Mom see Bess and Mick.
   ⬭ Mom sees Bess and Mick.

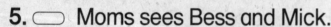

Home Activity Your child reviewed verbs that end in -s that describe what one person or thing does. Have your child create sentences about one person and more than one person, using correct verbs.

© Pearson Education 1

Name _____

Use the word in ( ) to finish each sentence.
Write it on the line.
Add -ing if needed.

Dad is **looking** for birds.
Dad and Bob **see** a tree.

(watch)

_____
- -

1. Dad is _____ the tree.

(help)

_____
- -

2. Bob is _____ him.

(spot)

_____
- -

3. Dad and Bob _____ a nest.

(eat)

_____
- -

4. The bird is _____.

Find the sentence that tells about the picture.
Mark the ⬭ to show your answer.

5. ⬭ Mom is missing Bob.
   ⬭ Mom is miss Bob.
   ⬭ Mom missing Bob.

Home Activity Your child reviewed adding -ing to verbs. Have your child use each verb from this page in a story about a different wild animal.

Practice Book Unit 1   **Phonics** Inflected Ending -ing Review **49**

Name _____

Pick words from the box that belong to each list.
Write the words in the lists.

yellow	three	green	blue	five
red	six	two	one	four

Colors

_____

1. _____

_____

2. _____

_____

3. _____

_____

4. _____

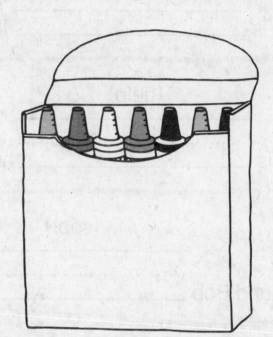

Numbers

1. _____

2. _____

3. _____

4. _____

5. _____

6. _____

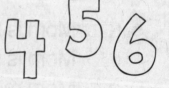

Home Activity Your child learned to make a list of things that belong together. Help your child make a list of his or her favorite foods or activities.

© Pearson Education 1

Here are ways to help your child practice skills while having fun!

Family Times

You are your child's first and best teacher!

This week we're

Reading Animal Park

Talking About Where animals live

Learning About Short *u*
  Final Blends
  Cause and Effect

Day 1

Have your child use a paper bag to make a bug puppet. Write these words on cards: *run, rug, rut, bug, bun, bus, jump, just, mud, must.* Invite your child to have the bug puppet read aloud each word.

Day 2

Write each word on a card: *dust, duck, dock, bump, jump, lump, lamp, limp, mist, mast, cast, dump, damp, camp, fist, fast.* Find different ways three or more words are alike, such as having the same beginning letter.

Day 3

Write the following words in a list: *home, into, many, them.* Have your child dictate a sentence for you to write. Then ask your child to read the sentences back to you. Together, illustrate one of the sentences.

Day 4

Write each spelling word on a card: *run, cut, must, sun, up, bump, jump, bus, nut, rug.* Sort the words into *things, actions,* and *"other words."*

Day 5

This week your child is learning the difference between cause and effect. As you go through your day together, discuss the events you see and what might have caused them or what their effect might be.

Materials index cards, markers

Game Directions

1. Together, copy the words on page 3 to index cards.

2. Shuffle the cards and divide them among players.

3. The first player chooses one of his or her cards and silently acts out the word. The remaining players must guess the word. The player to correctly guess the word gets to act out the next word. Continue play until all the cards have been used.

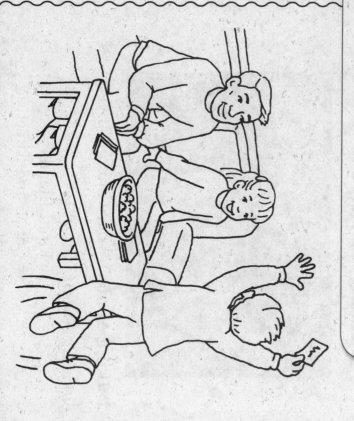

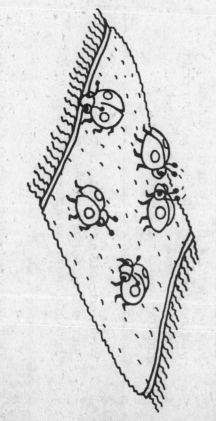

run	duck	mug
tug	up	dug
cut	bump	jug
gum	jump	rug
sun	bus	bug

Name _____

Say the word for each picture.
Write u on the line if you hear the **short u** sound.

p<u>u</u>p

1.

b _____ g

2.

d _____ ck

3.

b _____ s

4.

h _____ g

5.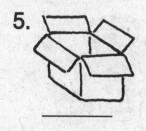

b _____ x

6.

dr _____ m

7.

s _____ n

8.

sl _____ d

Find the word that has the same middle sound as .
Mark the ⬭ to show your answer.

9. ⬭ mad
⬭ mud
⬭ mill

10. ⬭ plan
⬭ plot
⬭ plum

© Pearson Education 1

 School + Home   **Home Activity** Your child reviewed words with the short *u* sound heard in *pup*. Work with your child to write words that rhyme with *rug*.

Name _____

Look at the picture that shows what happened.
Circle the picture that shows why it happened.

Look at the picture that shows what happened.
Draw a picture that shows why it happened.

© Pearson Education 1

Home Activity Your child learned about cause (why something happens) and effect (what happens). Look for cause and effect with your child. For example, you might point out that when the temperature drops in the fall, frost forms.

Name _____

Say the word for each picture.
Circle the letters that finish each word.
Write the letters on the line.

 ne**st**

---

nd   nt

1. po _____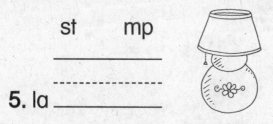

nt   mp

2. ju _____

---

mp   nt

3. de _____

st   nt

4. ca _____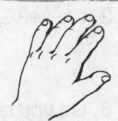

---

st   mp

5. la _____

nt   nd

6. ha _____

---

st   nt

7. ve _____

nt   mp

8. te _____

---

nt   st

9. fi _____

mp   st

10. sta _____

Home Activity Your child learned final consonant blends such as *mp*, *nd*, *nt*, and *st*. Have your child make up sentences using words from this page.

© Pearson Education 1

Name _____

Pick a word from the box to finish each sentence.
Write it on the line.

| home | into | many | them |

1. This is a _____ for _____ .

2. We see _____ .

3. Do you see _____ ?

4. The _____ go _____ the home.

Draw a picture of you going into your home.

5.

Home Activity Your child learned to read the words *home, into, many,* and *them.* Invite your child to use the words to describe life in his or her home.

Name _____

Circle a word to finish each sentence.
Write it on the line.

many   home

_____

----

1. We see the animals at _____.

many   into

_____

----

2. They use _____ logs.

park   zebras

_____

----

3. The birds are at the _____.

many   into

_____

----

4. The hippos go _____ the pond.

zebras   elephants

_____

----

5. Do you see the _____?

them   home

_____

----

6. We see _____ eating.

Home Activity Your child learned to read the words *elephants, hippos, home, into, many, park, them,* and *zebras.* Help your child make up a story about a day at the zoo using these words.

© Pearson Education 1

Name _____

Circle the word for each picture.
Write it on the line.

 ve_t_

1.

   bell   bill

   _____
   - - - - - - - - - - -

2.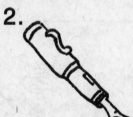

   pin   pen

   _____
   - - - - - - - - - - -

3.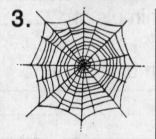

   web   won

   _____
   - - - - - - - - - - -

4.

   jug   jet

   _____
   - - - - - - - - - - -

5.

   bad   bed

   _____
   - - - - - - - - - - -

6.

   net   not

   _____
   - - - - - - - - - - -

7.

   pet   pit

   _____
   - - - - - - - - - - -

8.

   leg   log

   _____
   - - - - - - - - - - -

Find the word that has the same vowel sound as  .
Mark the ⬭ to show your answer.

9. ⬭ slug
   ⬭ slam
   ⬭ sled

10. ⬭ beg
    ⬭ bag
    ⬭ bug

 School + Home   **Home Activity** Your child reviewed words with the short *e* sound heard in *vet*. Help your child write a silly poem in which all the rhyming words have the short *e* sound. Encourage your child to read the poem aloud to family members.

© Pearson Education 1

Name _____

Circle the word for each picture.

black

1.
block
flock

2.
slant
plant

3.
flag
drag

4.
slip
drip

5.
drop
crop

6.
cluck
truck

7.
spill
drill

8.
trunk
skunk

Find the word that has the same beginning sound as the picture.
Mark the ⬭ to show your answer.

9. ⬭ flip
⬭ clip
⬭ trip

10. ⬭ clap
⬭ trot
⬭ step

School + Home **Home Activity** Your child reviewed words with initial blends *(flag, dress, sled)*. Have your child make up a sentence using two or more of the same blend. *(The slug slid down the slope.)*

© Pearson Education 1

Name _____

Look at the calendar. **Read** the questions.
Mark the ⬭ to show each answer.

SEPTEMBER

Sunday	Monday	Tuesday	Wednesday	Thursday	Friday	Saturday
						1
2	3	4	5	6	7	8
9	10	11	12	13	14	15
16	17	18	19	20	21	22
23	24	25	26	27	28	29
30						

1. How many days are in a week?
   ⬭ 6   ⬭ 7   ⬭ 30

2. What day is the 5th?
   ⬭ Saturday   ⬭ Wednesday   ⬭ Tuesday

3. How many Sundays are in this month?
   ⬭ 3   ⬭ 4   ⬭ 5

4. How many Wednesdays are in this month?
   ⬭ 3   ⬭ 4   ⬭ 5

Home Activity Your child learned to interpret information in a calendar. Display a calendar at home and discuss with your child how many days remain until an upcoming event.

© Pearson Education 1

Family Times

Name

You are your child's first and best teacher!

This week we're

Reading A Big Fish for Max

Max and Ruby

A Big Fish for Max

written and designed by Rosemary Wells

illustrated by Jody Wheeler

Where will Max get a big fish?

Talking About What a family does together

Learning About Digraphs *sh*, *th*
Vowel Sound in *ball*
Main Idea

Here are ways to help your child practice skills while having fun!

Day 1

Write these words on cards: *ship, shop, thin, than, dish, dash, with, moth.* Mix the cards. Have your child read aloud each word and raise his or her left hand for the *sh* sound and right hand for the *th* sound.

Day 2

Write each word on a card: *ball, call, fall, hall, mall, tall, wall, talk, walk.* Have your child use as many of the words as possible in a silly story about a very long walk.

Day 3

Have your child read the following words: *catch, good, no, put, want.* Then have him or her describe an exciting sporting scene, using one or all of the words.

Day 4

List the spelling words on paper: *ship, fish, then, shut, with, rush, shell, shop, trash, thin.* Have your child copy each word, writing the *sh* or *th* in red, the vowels in blue, and the remaining letters in green.

Day 5

This week your child is learning about the big idea in a story. As you read stories together, discuss what the author's big idea is for the story.

Materials crayons

Game Directions

1. Players take turns reading the words on the ship.
2. If the word has a *sh* sound, the player colors the space red.
3. If the word has a *th* sound, the player colors the space brown.

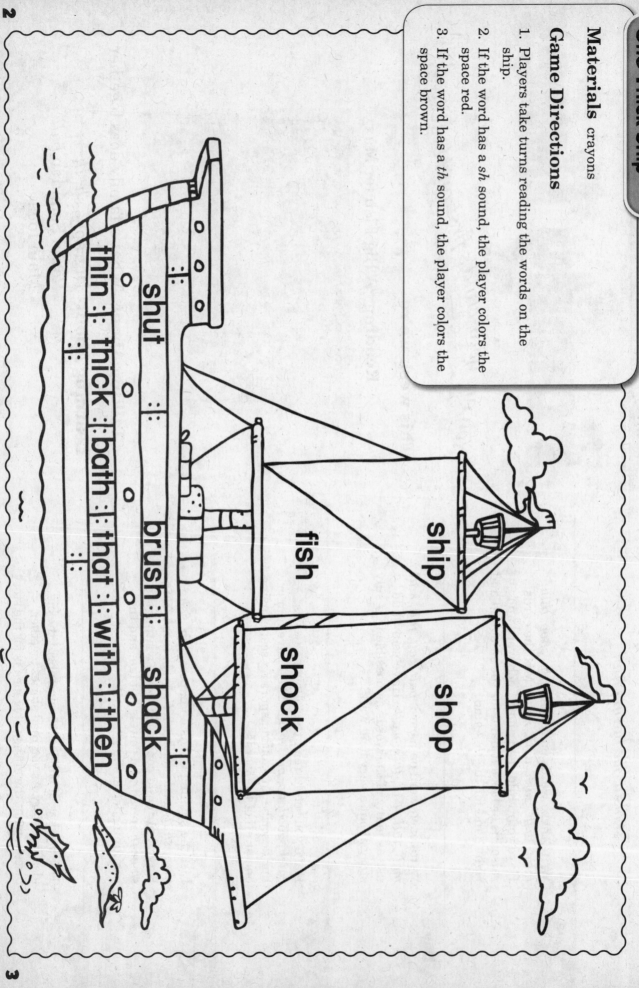

ship

fish

shop

shock

shut :: brush :: shack

thin :: thick :: bath :: that :: with :: then

Name _____

Say the word for each picture.
Write **sh** or **th** to finish each word.

di**sh**

think

1.

_____

- - - - - - - - - - - - - - -

_____ op

2.

_____

- - - - - - - - - - - - - - -

fi _____

3.

_____

- - - - - - - - - - - - - - -

_____ in

4.

_____

- - - - - - - - - - - - - - -

_____ ell

5.

_____

- - - - - - - - - - - - - - -

ba _____

6.

_____

- - - - - - - - - - - - - - -

bru _____

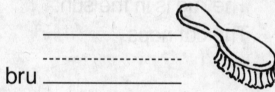

7.

_____

- - - - - - - - - - - - - - -

pa _____

8.

_____

- - - - - - - - - - - - - - -

tra _____

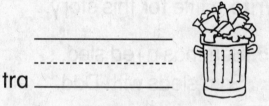

9.

_____

- - - - - - - - - - - - - - -

_____ ick

10.

_____

- - - - - - - - - - - - - - -

_____ ip

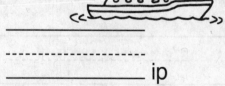

School + Home

Home Activity Your child added the digraphs *th* and *sh* (two letters that together stand for one sound) to complete words. Have your child copy the words that contain *sh* from this page and use as many of those words as possible in one sentence. Repeat using the *th* words.

Practice Book Unit 2

Phonics Digraphs sh, th **63**

© Pearson Education 1

Name _____

Read the story.
Circle the sentence that tells what the story is all about.
Draw a picture that shows what the story is about.

1. Pat runs and skips.   2.
   Pat jumps rope.
   Pat hits with a bat.
   Pat likes to play.

3. The cat likes to nap   4.
   in the sun.
   The cat is on the rug.
   The rug is in the sun.
   The cat naps.

Write a title for this story.

5. Sam has a red sled.
   Sam sleds with Dad.
   They hit a bump.
   Sam is not on the sled.

_____

- -

© Pearson Education 1

School + Home **Home Activity** Your child learned about the main idea of a story. As you read stories with your child, have your child tell you what the story is all about.

Name _____

Circle a word to finish each sentence.
Write it on the line.

 ball

mall   mill

_____
- - - - - - - - - - - - - - - - - - - -

1. We met Dad at the _____.

well   walk

_____
- - - - - - - - - - - - - - - - - - - -

2. We take a _____ and talk.

tell   tall

_____
- - - - - - - - - - - - - - - - - - - -

3. Dad got a _____ bag.

all   ill

_____
- - - - - - - - - - - - - - - - - - - -

4. We _____ go in.

smell   small

_____
- - - - - - - - - - - - - - - - - - - -

5. I am too _____ to see!

© Pearson Education 1

 School + Home **Home Activity** Your child practiced reading words with the vowel sound heard in *ball* and *walk*. Work with your child to write a list of words that rhyme with *ball*.

Name _____

Pick a word from the box to finish each sentence.
Write it on the line.

| catch | good | no | put | want |

---

1. Dad and Bob _____ to fish.

---

2. You can _____ it here.

---

3. Bob has _____ fish yet.

---

4. Bob can _____ that fish!

---

5. It is a _____ fish.

School + Home **Home Activity** Your child learned to read the words *catch, good, no, put,* and *want.* As you read with your child, encourage him or her to point out these words in print.

© Pearson Education 1

Name _____

Pick a word from the box to finish each sentence.
Write it on the line.

> catch   good   no   put   want

_____
- - - - - - - - - - - - - - - - - - - -
1. Do you _____ to play?

_____
- - - - - - - - - - - - - - - - - - - -
2. _____ on your hat.

_____
- - - - - - - - - - - - - - - - - - - -
3. That was a _____ hit.

_____
- - - - - - - - - - - - - - - - - - - -
4. Did you _____ the ball?

_____
- - - - - - - - - - - - - - - - - - - -
5. _____, I did not catch the ball.

Home Activity Your child learned to read the words *catch, good, no, put,* and *want.* Help your child use the words to write a story about what families do together or ways family members help each other.

© Pearson Education 1

Name _____

Circle the word for each picture.
Write it on the line.

 m<u>u</u>g

1.

bus   bass

_____

2.

cap   cup

_____

3.

duck   deck

_____

4.

lump   lamp

_____

5.

drag   drum

_____

6.

track   truck

_____

7.

tub   tab

_____

8.

stump   stamp

_____

Find the word that has the same vowel sound as .
Mark the ⬭ to show your answer.

9. ⬭ cab
   ⬭ cub
   ⬭ cob

10. ⬭ stick
    ⬭ stack
    ⬭ stuck

© Pearson Education 1

 School + Home **Home Activity** Your child reviewed words with the short *u* sound heard in *mug*. Work together to write a poem using as many of the short *u* words shown above as you can.

Name _____

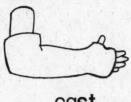 ca<u>st</u>  pla<u>nt</u>  ha<u>nd</u>  stu<u>mp</u>

Pick the letters from the box to finish each word.
Write the letters on the line.

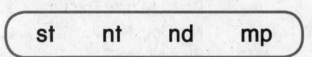 st   nt   nd   mp

1. 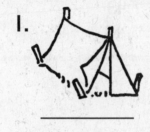 te _____
2.  sa _____
3.  sta _____
4.  li _____

5.  po _____
6.  ju _____
7. de _____
8. 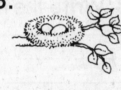 ne _____

Find the word that has the same ending sound as the picture.
Mark the ⬭ to show your answer.

9. ⬭ lamp ⬭ last ⬭ land
10. ⬭ stand ⬭ rent ⬭ rust

 School + Home **Home Activity** Your child reviewed words with final consonant blends *st, nt, nd,* and *mp*. Pick one final consonant blend such as *st* or *nd*. Have your child name as many words ending with that sound as possible.

Name _____

Ned's New Dog
Contents

1. Draw a circle around the page numbers.

2. Put a **box** around the chapter titles.

3. Write the name of the last chapter.

_____

- -

_____

4. Write the page number on which "Ned's New Plan" begins.

_____

- - - - - - - - - - - - - - - - -

_____

5. Write the total number of chapters in "Ned's New Dog."

_____

- - - - - - - - - - - - - - - - -

_____

© Pearson Education 1

Home Activity Your child learned to use the table of contents in a storybook to find information. As you read together, point out the table of contents and encourage your child to help you find information such as the page number for a specific chapter.

Family Times

You are your child's first and best teacher!

This week we're

Reading The Farmer in the Hat

The Farmer in the Hat
by Pat Cummings

Talking About How we learn together at school

Learning About Long *a* (CVCe)
c/s/ and *g*/j/
Cause and Effect

Here are ways to help your child practice skills while having fun!

Day 1

Make sock puppets. Write these words on cards: *lake, rake, face, gate, came, shape, wave, tape, cape.* Invite your child to have the sock puppet read each word.

Day 2

Write each word on a card: *cake, cat, cent, space, came, lace, gave, go, get, cage, gem, rage, page.* Have your child sort the cards into four piles: *c* as in *cake, c* as in *cent, g* as in *got,* and *g* as in *gem,* and then read them.

Day 3

Write the following words in a list: *be, could, horse, old, paper.* Together, make up a play about an old horse and an important paper.

Day 4

Write the spelling words: *face, made, age, safe, take, make, cage, cake, late, name.* Have your child rewrite them using one color crayon for the *a*'s, one color for the *e*'s, and a third color for the other letters.

Day 5

This week your child is learning about cause and effect. Discuss events throughout your day and what might have caused them or what their effect might be.

The Plate Game

Materials index cards, marker, plate

Game Directions

1. Cut small index cards into six small rectangles and use the chart below to create letter cards. Copy the words on page 3 onto a piece of lined paper.

2. Shuffle the letter cards and give each player five cards. Place the remaining cards face down on a plate.

3. Players look at their cards and try to build words from the list. As each word is made, that word is crossed off the list. Players take turns asking other players for a missing letter. If that person has the letter, he or she must give it to the asking player. If that person does not have the letter, he or she tells the player to "Go to the plate" to collect another letter card. Play continues until all the words have been formed.

Game Cards Needed

Number of cards needed	1 of each	2 of each	3 of each	5 of each	10
Letters	F, G, M, N, R, Sh, W, V	C, K, T	L	P	A, E

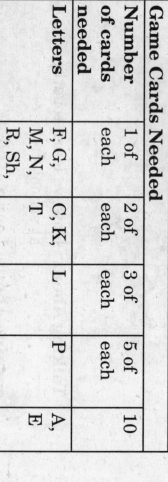

lake	plane
rake	face
game	shape
wave	tape
plate	cape

Name _____

Circle the word for each picture.

 c<u>a</u>ke

---

1.

rake   rack

2.

snack   snake

3.

frog   frame

4.

can   cane

5.

cape   cap

6.

plane   plan

7.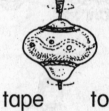

lock   lake

8.

tape   top

9.

wave   wag

10.

skit   skate

11.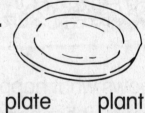

plate   plant

12.

shape   shop

13.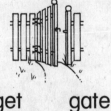

get   gate

14.

game   gum

15.

van   vase

 School + Home

Home Activity Your child practiced reading words with the long *a* sound that follow a consonant-vowel-consonant-*e* pattern, such as *cake*. Work with your child to write a list of words that rhyme with *cake*. Repeat with *cave*.

© Pearson Education 1

Name _____

Look at the first picture that shows what happened.
Circle the picture that shows why it happened.

1.

2.

3.

4.

Look at the picture that shows what happened.
Draw a picture that shows why it happened.

5.

Home Activity Your child learned about cause (why something happens) and effect (what happens). Call your child's attention to causes and effects by asking questions such as: *What happened?* (effect) *Why did it happen?* (cause)

© Pearson Education 1

Name

Circle the word for each picture.
Write it on the line.

 la<u>c</u>e

 a<u>g</u>e

1.

face   fake

2.

rake   race

3.

cave   cage

4.

wag   wage

5.

speck   space

6.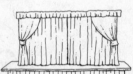

stage   stake

7.

track   trace

8.

pace   page

Find the word that has the same ending sound as the picture.
Mark the ⬭ to show your answer.

9. ⬭ brave
   ⬭ brace
   ⬭ brake

10. ⬭ rag
    ⬭ race
    ⬭ rage

 School + Home **Home Activity** Your child practiced reading and writing words that have the sound that *c* stands for in *lace* and the sound that *g* stands for in *age*. Ask your child to write a list of words that rhyme with *lace* and a list of words that rhyme with *age*.

© Pearson Education 1

Name _____

Pick a word from the box to finish each sentence.
Write it on the line.

be	could	horse	old	paper

1. Dad gave me a _____ .

2. She was not _____ .

3. She _____ run and jump.

4. I put her name on a _____ .

5. We will _____ pals!

School + Home

Home Activity Your child learned to read the words *be, could, horse, old,* and *paper*. Write these words on small pieces of paper or self-stick notes. Tape them on a mirror or desk for your child to practice every day.

© Pearson Education 1

Name _____

Pick a word from the box to finish each sentence.
Write it on the line.

> be   could   farmer
> horse   old   paper

_____
- -
1. Mr. MacDonald is a _____ .

_____
- -
2. He has a _____ .

_____
- -
3. His _____ gerbil is in a cage.

_____
- -
4. It likes to rip up _____ and squeak .

_____
- -
5. _____ the cat get in the cage?

_____
- -
6. No, the pet will _____ safe.

Home Activity Your child learned to read the words *be, could, farmer, gerbil, horse, MacDonald, squeak,* and *old.* Ask your child to make up a story using these words. Help him or her to write the story and draw a picture about it.

Name _____

Look at each picture.
Circle the word to finish each sentence.
Write it on the line.

 **sh**ip    **th**in

trash   track   trap

_____

1. Pick up all the _____ .

rug   rub   rush

_____

2. Do not _____ to the bus.

pat   path   pass

_____

3. Walk on the _____ .

math   mat   mash

_____

4. Do all the _____ .

self   shelf   shell

_____

5. Put the dish on the _____ .

Home Activity Your child reviewed words with *sh* and *th*. Take turns with your child naming as many words beginning with *sh* as you can. Repeat with *th*.

Name _____

Circle the word for each picture.
Write it on the line.

 b<u>a</u>ll

---

1.

call   cape

_____

2.

tell   tall

_____

3.

bell   ball

_____

4.

walk   wake

_____

5.

fill   fall

_____

6.

stack   stall

_____

7.

hall   hill

_____

8.

take   talk

_____

Find the word that has the same middle sound as .
Mark the ⬭ to show your answer.

9. ⬭ stalk
    ⬭ stake
    ⬭ stack

10. ⬭ smell
     ⬭ small
     ⬭ snake

 School + Home   **Home Activity** Your child practiced reading words with the vowel sound heard in *ball* and *walk*. Copy on cards each of the *all* and *alk* words from this page. Then have your child sort the cards according to sounds and read the words aloud.

© Pearson Education 1

Name _____

Read the poster.
Write the answers.

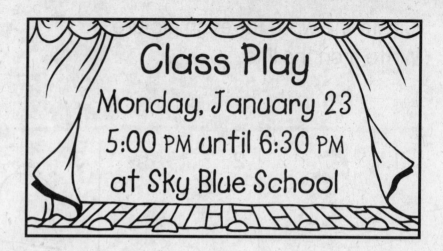

Class Play
Monday, January 23
5:00 PM until 6:30 PM
at Sky Blue School

1. What event does the poster tell about?

_____

_____

2. What time is the event?

_____

_____

3. On what day of the week is the event?

_____

_____

4. Where is the event?

_____

_____

5. What is the date of the event?

_____

_____

© Pearson Education 1

School + Home **Home Activity** Your child learned to find information on an announcement poster. As you see similar announcements, read them together and have your child find the important information.

Family Times

You are your child's first and best teacher!

This week we're

Reading Who Works Here?

Who Works Here!

by Melissa Blackwell Burke
Illustrated by Tim Spransy

Who works where you live!

Talking About Who makes our neighborhood
a nice place to live

Learning About Long *i* (CVCe)
Digraphs *wh, ch, tch*
Author's Purpose

---

*Here are ways to help your child practice
skills while having fun!*

Day 1

Do a rhyming activity. Say one of the following
words and have your child think of a word that
rhymes with it: *hike, wide, while, lime, fine, mice.*

Day 2

On cards, write *white, wham, whack, check,
chin, chat, batch, latch, itch, stitch, fetch.*
Write *wh, ch,* and *tch* each on separate cards.
Have your child sort the words under the
matching word-part cards and read them.

Day 3

Write these words: *live, out, people, who, work.*
Together, write a poem about people in your
neighborhood. Read the poem together and
have your child underline the list words.

Day 4

Write each spelling word on a card: *like, ride,
smile, time, white, bike, dime, hide, ice, kite.*
Have your child sort the words into groups of
words that rhyme and "other" words.

Day 5

This week your child is learning about why
an author wrote a story, such as to inform
or entertain. As you read a story, discuss the
author's purpose for writing it.

Fire! Fire!

Materials red and yellow crayons

Game Directions

1. Players take turns reading the words on the fire truck.
2. If the word has a *long i* sound, the player colors the space red.
3. If the word has a *short i* sound, the player colors the space yellow.

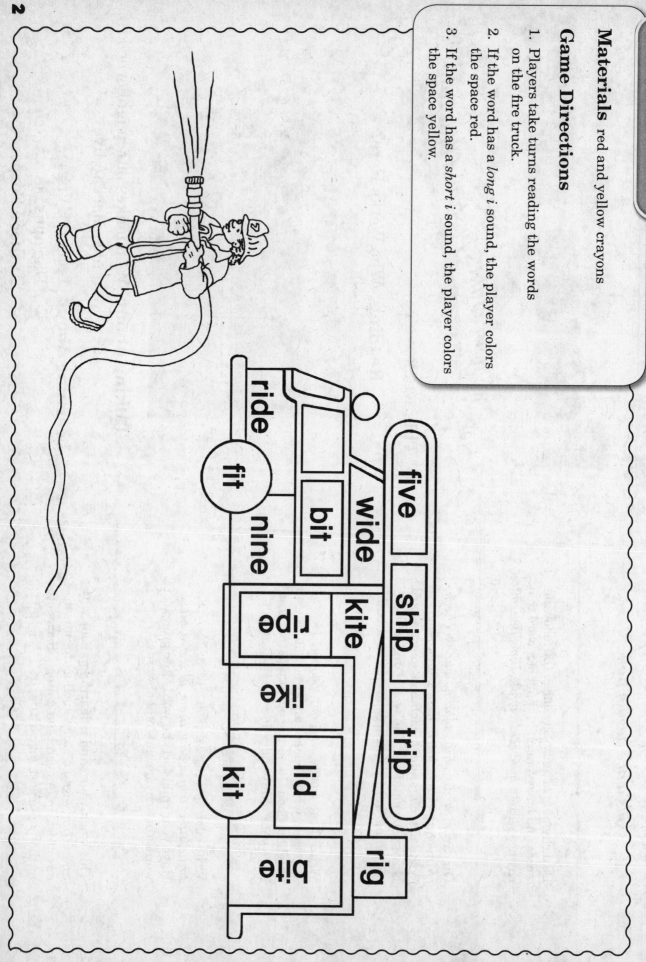

Name _____

Circle the word for each picture.

9 nine

1.

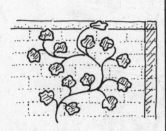

vine   vane

2.

mane   mice

3.

wig   wipe

4.

bike   bill

5.

pill   pile

6.

slide   slid

7.

fish   file

8.

shine   shin

Find the word that has the same **long i** sound as  .

Mark the ⬭ to show your answer.

9. ⬭ flip
   ⬭ fine
   ⬭ fin

10. ⬭ slid
   ⬭ sip
   ⬭ slice

© Pearson Education 1

Home Activity Your child practiced reading words with the long *i* sound that follow a consonant-vowel-consonant-*e* pattern, such as *nine*. Work with your child to write a list of words that rhyme with *nine*. Repeat with *hide*.

Name _____

Circle the five books that may tell you about something real.

1.

2.

3.

4.

5.

6.

7.

8.

9.

Think of a book that tells you about something real.

Write its name on the line.

Draw a picture in the box that shows what the book is about.

10. _____

11.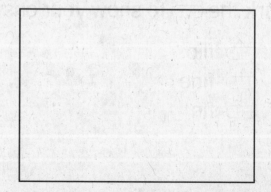

Home Activity Your child learned to tell what a book might be about by figuring out why it was written. As you read various materials with your child, ask what he or she thinks each is about and why the author wrote it.

© Pearson Education 1

Name _____

Circle the word for each picture.

 **wh**isk   **ch**ick    **itch**

1. 	2. 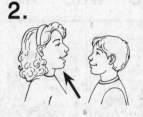	3. 	4. 
wall whale	shin chin	catch cats	wash watch

5. 	6. ✓	7. 	8. 
ship whip	chick check	patch pass	limp chimp

Draw a picture for each word.

9. chase

10. pitch

Home Activity Your child practiced reading words with digraphs *wh*, *ch*, and *tch* (letters that together stand for one sound). Have your child use each word above in a sentence.

© Pearson Education 1

Name _____

Pick a word from the box to finish each sentence.
Write it on the line. **Remember** to use capital letters at the beginning of a sentence.

live   out   people   who   work

1. _____ can fix this clock?

2. The _____ in the shop can fix it.

3. They will _____ on it.

4. Where does your dog _____ ?

5. His home is _____ here.

Home Activity Your child learned to read the words *live, out, people, who,* and *work*. Point to these words on the page. Have your child read each word and use it in a spoken sentence.

Name _____

Pick a word from the box to match each clue.
Write it in the puzzle.

| live | mail | out | people | who | work |

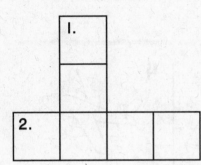

1. _____ is in this busy neighborhood?

2. not play

3. Do you _____ in that home?

4. He will _____ the gift.

5. Many _____ live and work here.

6. not in

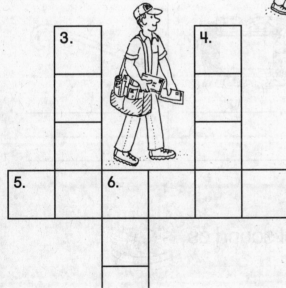

© Pearson Education 1

Home Activity Your child learned to read the words *busy, live, mail, neighborhood, out, people, who,* and *work.* Help your child make up a short story using some of these words. Write the story. Have your child draw a picture to go with it.

Name _____

Pick a word from the box to match each picture.
Write it on the line.

cage   cane   face   frame   lake   plane   scale   snake

1.

_____

2.

_____

3.

_____

4.

_____

5.

_____

6.

_____

7.

_____

8.

_____

Find the word that has the same vowel sound as .
Mark the ⬭ to show your answer.

9. ⬭ tap
   ⬭ tape
   ⬭ trap

10. ⬭ plan
    ⬭ place
    ⬭ pan

© Pearson Education 1

School + Home

Home Activity Your child reviewed words with the long *a* sound as in *cape*. Write *face* on a sheet of paper. Have your child change the beginning consonant to write a new long *a* word, such as *race*. Continue changing letters and building new words.

Name _____

Look at each picture.
Circle the word to finish each sentence.
Write it on the line.

 la**c**e

 ca**g**e

---

place   plants   planes

_____

- -

1. This is a good _____ to shop.

---

stag   stack   stage

_____

- -

2. They will act on _____ .

---

came   cage   cave

_____

- -

3. She sells mice in a _____ .

---

rack   rake   race

_____

- -

4. He will run in the big _____ .

---

slid   slice   slick

_____

- -

5. She will sell you a _____ of cake.

School + Home **Home Activity** Your child practiced reading and writing words that have the sound that *c* stands for in *lace* and the sound that *g* stands for in *age*. Work with your child to think of pairs of rhyming words for each word answer above.

© Pearson Education 1

Name _____

Look at the map.

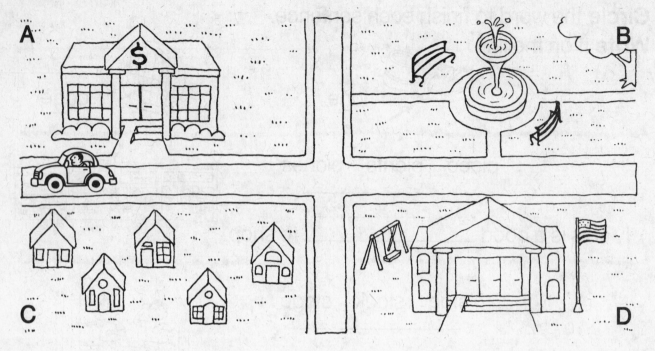

1. **Circle** the school.

2. **Draw** a box around the bank.

3. **Underline** the park.

4. **Write** the number of houses on block C.

_____

- - - - - - - - - - - - - - - -

_____

5. **Write** the number of cars on the map.

_____

- - - - - - - - - - - - - - - -

_____

Home Activity Your child learned to use a map to gather information. Point out maps as you see them and challenge your child to point out places featured on the maps.

Family Times

Name

You are your child's first and best teacher!

Here are ways to help your child practice skills while having fun!

This week we're

Reading The Big Circle

Who lived here long ago?

Talking About How animals work together to survive

Learning About Long *o* (CVCe)
Contractions *n't*, *'m*, *'ll*
Sequence of Events

Day 1

On a large piece of paper, write – o – e. Make these letter cards: *c, h, m, n, p, r, s, t, v, w.* Write the following words: *note, vote, wove, cove, pose, rose, hope, mope.* Take turns placing the correct letter in each blank to form each of the words on the list.

Day 2

Write each of these contractions and the words that make them on separate cards: *I'm, we'll, you'll, can't, haven't, I am, we will, you will, can not, have not.* Mix up the cards and have your child match them.

Day 3

Write the following words in a list: *down, inside, now, there, together.* Ask your child to read each word and say its opposite.

Day 4

Write each spelling word on a card: *home, hope, rose, woke, those, bone, hose, joke, rode, stone.* Have your child sort the words into two groups: *things you can touch* and *things you can't touch.*

Day 5

This week your child is learning about the order in which events occur in a story. As you read together, have your child tell you what happened first, next, and last in the story.

Make a Match

Materials cards, marker

Game Directions

1. Make twelve picture cards similar to the ones shown of the following rhyming words: *home, dome; broke, yoke; bone, cone, smoke, rope, slope; rose, nose.*

2. Shuffle the cards and place them face down in a pile between you.

3. Each player begins by picking two cards. If words on the cards rhyme, the player puts them aside. Play then passes to the next player.

4. Play continues until all cards are gone. The player with the most pairs wins!

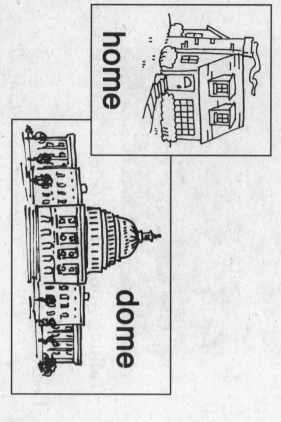

home

dome

smoke

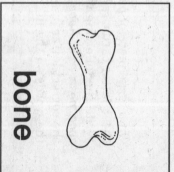

bone

cone

nose

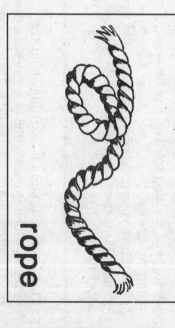

rope

Name _____

Circle the word for each picture.

 r**o**pe

---

1.	2.	3.	4.

snake smoke	rod rose	globe glob	cone cane

5.	6.	7.	8.
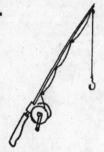	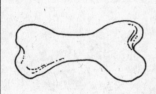		
rode rod	bond bone	stove stop	not note

Find the word that has the same **long o** sound as .
Mark the ⬭ to show your answer.

9. ⬭ mile
   ⬭ mole
   ⬭ mill

10. ⬭ hip
    ⬭ hop
    ⬭ hope

School + Home **Home Activity** Your child practiced reading words with the long *o* sound that follow a consonant-vowel-consonant-*e* pattern, such as *rope*. Work with your child to write a list of words that rhyme with *bone*. Repeat with *joke*.

© Pearson Education 1

Name _____

Write a number in each box to show the right order.

1. ☐

2. ☐

3. ☐

Look at each picture.
Draw what will happen next.

4.

5.

 Home Activity Your child learned about the order in which things happen in a story. After you read a story with your child, have your child tell you what happened first, next, and last in the story.

Name _____

Read each sentence.
Write the contraction for the underlined words.

I **do not** think I can do this.   I **don't** think I can do this.

_____

1. "I <u>can not</u> make a nest," said the little bird.   _____

2. "<u>I will</u> need help with the sticks," said
the little bird.   _____

_____

3. "I <u>do not</u> think I can help," said the frog.   _____

4. "<u>You will</u> need a big bird to help you,"
said the frog.   _____

5. "<u>I am</u> a big bird! I can help," said
the big bird.   _____

Home Activity Your child combined words to form contractions ending with *n't*, *'m*, and *'ll*. Say a
contraction aloud. Have your child tell you the two words that were combined to make the contraction.
Repeat with the other contractions.

© Pearson Education 1

Name _____

Pick a word from the box to match each clue.
Write it on the line.

down   inside   now   there   together

1. not up

_____

_____

2. not here

_____

_____

3. not outside

_____

_____

4. not then

_____

_____

5. not one here and one there

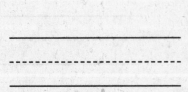

_____

_____

Home Activity Your child learned to read and write the words *down, inside, now, there,* and *together*. Read one word aloud. Have your child point to it and use it in a sentence. Repeat with the other words.

Name _____

Circle a word to finish each sentence.
Write it on the line.

down   herd

_____

----

1. The triceratops takes _____ the small tree.

circle   baby

_____

----

2. He is a _____ triceratops.

now   meat

_____

----

3. He is eating _____ .

baby   together

_____

----

4. The herd is _____ .

inside   outside

_____

----

5. They put the little ones _____ .

circle   there

_____

----

6. The triceratops baby is safe _____ .

Home Activity Your child learned to read and write the words *baby, circle, down, herd, inside, meat, now, there, together,* and *triceratops.* Help your child make up a short story using some of these words and then practice reading it aloud.

© Pearson Education 1

Name _____

Pick a word from the box to match each picture.
Write the word on the line.
Circle each picture whose name has the **long i** sound.

bike   dime   five   kid
mice   pig   slide   vine

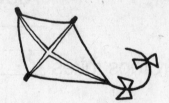 k<u>i</u>te

1. _____

2. _____

3. _____

4. _____

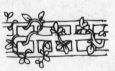

5. _____

6. _____

5

7. _____

8. _____

Home Activity Your child practiced reading words with the long *i* sound that follow a consonant-vowel-consonant-*e* pattern, such as *kite*. Work with your child to write a story using as many of the long *i* words listed above as possible.

© Pearson Education 1

Name _____

Pick a word from the box to match each picture.
Write it on the line.

> check   chin   chips   crutch
> switch   watch   whale   whisk

1.
_____

2.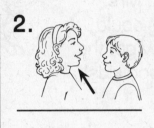
_____

3.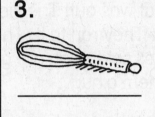
_____

4.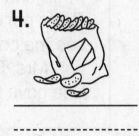
_____

5.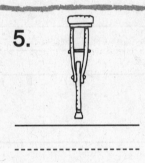
_____

6.
_____

7.
_____

8.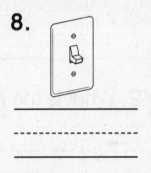
_____

Find the word that has the same beginning sound as the picture.
Mark the ⬭ to show your answer.

9. ⬭ chin
⬭ shin
⬭ thin

10. ⬭ ship
⬭ white
⬭ chip

School + Home

Home Activity Your child reviewed words with digraphs *wh*, *ch*, and *tch* (letters that together stand for one sound). Help your child make up a sentence that contains words that begin with *ch*, such as *The chick sat on a chair and ate chips.*

© Pearson Education 1

Name _____

Read the newsletter. **Answer** the questions.

The Neighborhood   March

Kids Help!
by Pam Ride

Jill and Sam went for a walk. Mrs. Bell's pet cat was out! The kids could see the cat. They ran to it. They got the cat. Mrs. Bell said, "You are good kids!" She gave them a hug.

---

1. What is the name of the newsletter?

_____

- -

_____

2. What is the name of the story?

_____

- -

_____

3. What is the story about?

_____

- -

_____

_____

- -

_____

Home Activity Your child learned to use a newsletter to get information. As you look at newsletters, newspapers, or magazines, point out the different kinds of type, such as bold or italic text. Discuss why the text looks different from the surrounding type.

© Pearson Education 1

Family Times

You are your child's first and best teacher!

This week we're

Reading Life in the Forest

What lives in the forest?

Life in the Forest

by Claire Daniel

Talking About How plants and animals live together

Learning About Long *u*, Long *e* (CVC*e*)
Inflected Ending -*ed*
Author's Purpose

Here are ways to help your child practice skills while having fun!

Day 1
Play a rhyming game. Write these words: *cute, mule, tune, tube, rule, cube, flute.* Ask your child to use the rhyming words to tell a story about two friends named Pete and Gene.

Day 2
Write each word on a card: *mix, mixed, pack, packed, end, ended, hand, handed, play, played, ask, asked.* Place the cards face down. Take turns flipping over two cards, trying to make a match.

Day 3
Write the following words in a list: *around, find, food, grow, under, water.* Together, write a story about life under water using the words.

Day 4
Write each spelling word on a card: *huge, June, rule, tube, use, cube, cute, flute, rude, mule.* Talk about ways you can sort the words into groups that make sense.

Day 5
This week your child is learning to think about why an author might have written a story. As you read together, stop and discuss the author's purpose.

Materials paper, markers, 1 coin

Game Directions

1. Make a large game board like the one shown.
2. Players take turns tossing the coin onto the game board and saying a long *u* word that begins with the letters shown in the square.
3. A correct answer earns the number of points shown in that square.
4. The first player to get 10 points wins!

cube

June

lute

flute

tube

dude

c 3	l 4	m 3
fl 2	t 2	t 4
J 2	d 3	f 2
pr 2	r 2	h 4

2

3

Name _____

Circle the word for each picture.

 cu̲be

I. 	2. 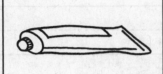	3. 	4. 
mule mile	tub tube	cub cube	Pete pet
5. 	6. 	7. 	8. 
tug tune	flat flute	tub tube	hug huge

Find the word that has the same **long u** sound as  .
Mark the ⬭ to show your answer.

9. ⬭ rut
   ⬭ rid
   ⬭ rule

10. ⬭ cut
    ⬭ cute
    ⬭ cup

© Pearson Education 1

 Home Activity Your child practiced reading words with the long *u* and long *e* sounds that follow a consonant-vowel-consonant-*e* pattern, such as *cube* and *Steve*. Write words from this page in a list. Say each word. Have your child point to the word and read it.

Name _____

Look at this book cover.
Circle or **write** your answers.

_____

1. Who wrote this book? _____

2. What do you think this book will be about?

   real dogs   silly dogs   a real trip

3. What do you think this book will be like?

   funny   sad   full of facts

4. Why do you think the writer wrote this book?

   to tell facts about dogs   to make you sad   to make you laugh

5. Would you want to read this book? Why or why not?

_____

_____

_____

© Pearson Education 1

Home Activity Your child learned to tell what a book might be about by figuring out why it was written. As you read various materials with your child, have your child tell you what he or she thinks each is about and why the author wrote it.

104 **Comprehension** Author's Purpose   Practice Book Unit 2

Name _____

Pick a word from the box to finish each sentence.
Add -ed to each word. **Write** it on the line.

call   walk   sniff   jump   rest

1. They _____ rope together.
_____

2. Pam _____ June.
_____

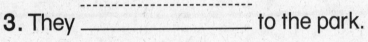

3. They _____ to the park.
_____

4. They _____ in the shade.
_____

5. They _____ the flowers.
_____

Home Activity Your child practiced writing words ending in -ed, like *patched*. Ask your child to read each word and use it in a sentence.

Practice Book Unit 2

Phonics Inflected Ending -ed **105**

Name _____

Look at each picture.
Read the words.
Write the word on the line that best fits the picture.

1.    find
   around
_____

2.    water
   food
_____

3. 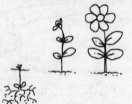   around
   under
_____

4.    grow
   find
_____

5.    water
   under
_____

6.   food
   water
_____

© Pearson Education 1

School + Home **Home Activity** Your child learned to read the words *around, find, food, grow, under,* and *water*. Make up clues for the words on this page. Ask your child to identify the words. Challenge your child to think of some clues too.

106 **High-Frequency Words**   **Practice Book Unit 2**

Name _____

Write a word from the box to finish each sentence.

> around find food grow under water

_____
----
1. The hummingbirds _____ food.

_____
----
2. The bears are _____ the bush.

_____
----
3. The squirrels eat _____ .

_____
----
4. The fox finds _____ .

_____
----
5. The woodpecker taps _____ the tree.

_____
----
6. The leaves _____ on trees.

School + Home **Home Activity** This week your child learned to read the words *around, bear, find, forest, food, grow, hummingbirds, leaves, squirrels, under, water,* and *woodpecker*. Give a clue for each word. Have your child point to the word and read it.

Name _____

Pick a word from the box to match each picture.
Write it on the line.

| bone   hole   home   nose   note   pole   robe   rope |

1.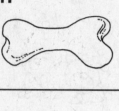

_____
- - - - - - - - - - -

2.

_____
- - - - - - - - - - -

3.

_____
- - - - - - - - - - -

4.

_____
- - - - - - - - - - -

5.

_____
- - - - - - - - - - -

6.

_____
- - - - - - - - - - -

7.

_____
- - - - - - - - - - -

8.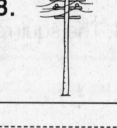

_____
- - - - - - - - - - -

Find the word that has the same vowel sound as .
Mark the ⬯ to show your answer.

9. ⬯ rod
⬯ rode
⬯ ride

10. ⬯ spoke
⬯ space
⬯ smock

 School + Home

Home Activity Your child reviewed words with the long *o* sound that follow the pattern consonant-vowel-consonant-*e* as in *bone*. Give a clue about each long *o* word shown above and challenge your child to guess it. For example: *What does a dog like to chew? (bone)*

Practice Book Unit 2

© Pearson Education 1

Name _____

Pick a contraction from the box to finish each sentence.
Write it on the line. **Remember** to use capital letters at the beginning of a sentence.

> can not = can't   do not = don't
> he will = he'll   is not = isn't

1. _____
   _____ jump on a rock.

2. He _____
   _____ find good food.

3. _____
   _____ eat that!

4. _____
   _____ this good?

Find the contraction for the two words.
Mark the ⬭ to show your answer.

5. I + am   ⬭ I'm
        ⬭ I'll
        ⬭ isn't

6. you + will   ⬭ I'm
          ⬭ you're
          ⬭ you'll

School + Home **Home Activity** Your child wrote contractions to finish sentences. Say one of the following word pairs and ask your child to combine them into a contraction: *could not, have not, was not, she will, I am* (couldn't, haven't, wasn't, she'll, I'm).

© Pearson Education 1

Name _____

A B C D E F G H I J K L M N O P Q R S T U V W X Y Z

Write the words from each box in ABC order.

| hip   top   play   sack |

1. _____

2. _____

3. _____

4. _____

| you   on   and   in |

5. _____

6. _____

7. _____

8. _____

Circle the word that is not in ABC order.

| cup   sand   lot   man |

Write the word that comes before lot.

9. _____

Write in order the two words that come after lot.

10. _____

11. _____

Home Activity Your child learned to find and arrange words in alphabetical order. Provide your child with words that he or she can read and write. Have your child write the words in ABC order.

© Pearson Education 1

Family Times

You are your child's first and best teacher!

This week we're

Reading Honey Bees

What happens inside a bee hive?

Honey Bees

Talking About How a community of insects is like a community of people

Learning About Long e: e, ee
Syllables VCCV
Compare and Contrast

Here are ways to help your child practice skills while having fun!

Day 1

Encourage your child to write a sentence that includes all of the following words: *we, see, bee, green, tree.* Invite your child to use a bee puppet to read aloud each word.

Day 2

Write these two-syllable words on cards: *basket, dinner, helmet, mitten, picnic, pencil, rabbit, walnut.* Cut the words apart between the two middle consonants and have your child match the syllables to make words.

Day 3

Write the following words in a list: *also, family, new, other, some, their.* Have your child dictate a sentence for each word. Write them and have your child read the sentences back to you. Together, draw a picture that illustrates one of the sentences.

Day 4

Write each spelling word on a card: *be, feet, he, see, we, green, me, she, tree, week.* Have your child sort the words according to number of vowels.

Day 5

This week your child is learning to look for similarities and differences in stories. As you read together, ask questions such as "How is this character like (or different from) the one we read about in the last book?"

Spin and Spell

Materials paper, scissors, paper clip, pencil, 1 button per player

Game Directions

1. Make a simple spinner as shown.
2. Players take turns spinning and then naming and spelling a word with the long *e* sound spelled either *ee* as in *tree* or *e* as in *we*. Words that could be used include: *be, he, me, she, we, bee, feet, free, green, keep, see, sleep, teeth, tree, week.*
3. If a player spells the word correctly, he or she moves that number of spaces.
4. The first player to reach the end wins!

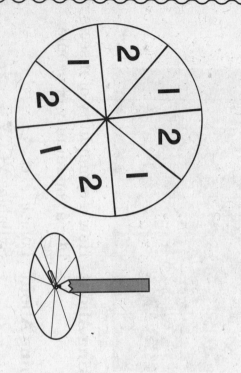

© Pearson Education 1

2

3

Name _____

Help the bee get home.
Read each word.
Draw a line that goes past only the **long e** words.
Write the **long e** words on the lines.

b<u>ee</u>

feet

bed

beet

wet

we

net

sheet

peel

jeep

he

jet

me

Home

1. _____

2. _____

3. _____

4. _____

5. _____

6. _____

7. _____

8. _____

© Pearson Education 1

Home Activity Your child practiced reading and writing words with the long e sound spelled e and ee as in *he* and *jeep*. Have your child make a list of words that rhyme with *seed*. Repeat with *jeep*.

Name _____

Look at both pictures.
Write sentences to tell how the pictures are the same and different.

Dee

Lee

Same

_____

1. _____

_____

2. _____

_____

Different

_____

3. _____

_____

4. _____

_____

5. _____

_____

© Pearson Education 1

Home Activity Your child used pictures to tell how two things are alike and different. Point out two objects or two pictures to your child. Encourage your child to tell you how they are the same and how they are different.

114 **Comprehension** Compare and Contrast

Name _____

Circle the word for each picture.

ki<u>tt</u>en

1.	2.	3.	4.

ramp rabbit	button brake	dinner dent	base basket

5.	6.	7.	8.

helmet hello	napkin name	mask muffin	wall walnut

Draw a picture for each word.

9. mitten

10. picnic

School + Home   **Home Activity** Your child read words with two syllables that have two consonants in the middle. Have your child choose five words from the page and use each word in a sentence.

Practice Book Unit 2   **Phonics** Syllables VCCV **115**

Name _____

Pick a word from the box to match each clue.
Write the words in the puzzles.

also family new other some their

1. not a lot

2. too

3.

4. not old

5. It's not this one. It's the _____ one.

6. It's not my food. It's _____ food.

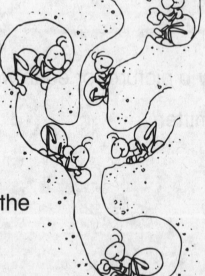

 School + Home **Home Activity** Your child learned to read the words *also, family, new, other, some,* and *their*. Help your child to make up a story or poem using these words. Work together to write the story or poem and read it to other family members.

© Pearson Education 1

Name _____

Pick a word from the box to complete each sentence.
Write it on the line. **Begin** each sentence with a capital letter.

> also   family   new   other   some   their

1. After cold days, bees from an old hive
   _____
   ----
   make a _____ one.

   _____
   ----

2. Bees in the hive work like a _____ .

   _____
   ----

3. Each bee helps the _____ bees.

   _____
   ----

4. Bees use _____ wings to fly to flowers.

   _____
   ----

5. _____ bees use nectar to make honey.

   _____
   ----

6. People _____ like honey.

Home Activity Your child learned the words *also, cold, family, flowers, honey, nectar, new, other, some,*
their, and *worker.* Help your child write a story using some of these words about a family that goes to live in
the forest.

© Pearson Education 1

Name _____

Look at each picture.
Circle the word to finish each sentence.
Write it on the line.

 c<u>u</u>be

---

flute   flop   flub
_____

- - - - - - - - - - - - - - - - - -

1. Steve plays the _____ .

---

mill   mule   mole
_____

- - - - - - - - - - - - - - - - - -

2. The _____ eats grass.

Pet   Put   Pete
_____

- - - - - - - - - - - - - - - - - -

3. _____ can use a rake.

---

cut   can   cute
_____

- - - - - - - - - - - - - - - - - -

4. June is a _____ cat.

---

tune   tube   tub
_____

- - - - - - - - - - - - - - - - - -

5. Use this _____ .

 Home Activity Your child reviewed words with the long *u* and the long *e* sounds that follow the pattern consonant-vowel-consonant-e as in *cube* or *Pete*. Work with your child to name pairs of rhyming words that have the long *u* sound.

© Pearson Education 1

Name _____

Bun watch<u>ed</u> a bug.

Add -ed to each word.
Write the new word.

look

want

1. _____

2. _____

sniff   rest   snack

3. _____ 4. _____ 5. _____

Use the words you wrote to finish the sentences.
Write the words on the lines.

6. Bun _____ grapes.

7. Bun _____ under a bush.

8. Bun _____ around.

9. Bun _____ on grapes.

10. Then Bun _____ .

Home Activity Your child added -ed to verbs. Read a storybook with your child and look for words that end in -ed. Have your child use each word you find in a new sentence.

© Pearson Education 1

Name _____

Look at the picture dictionary. **Follow** the directions.

   1. **Circle** the cat.

   2. **Make** a box around the dog.

Write the names of two things that fly.

3. _____

4. _____

Write the name of one thing that has two legs.

5. _____

© Pearson Education 1

 Home Activity Your child learned about the parts of a picture dictionary. Find a picture dictionary at the library and help your child use it to understand the meanings of related words.

120 **Research and Study Skills** Picture Dictionary   **Practice Book Unit 2**

Name _____

Computer Keyboard

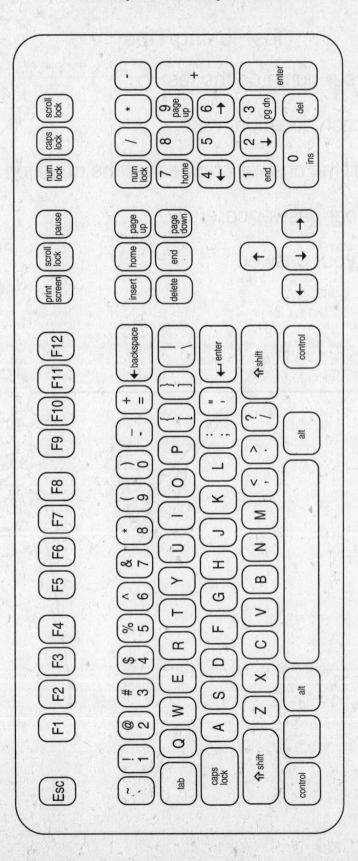

© Pearson Education 1

Name _____

Test-Taking Tips

1. Write your name on the test.

2. Read each question twice.

3. Read all the answer choices for the question.

4. Mark your answer carefully.

5. Check your answer.

Words I Can Now Read and Write

_____   _____
- - - - - - - - - - - - - - - - -   - - - - - - - - - - - - - - - - -
_____   _____
- - - - - - - - - - - - - - - - -   - - - - - - - - - - - - - - - - -
_____   _____
- - - - - - - - - - - - - - - - -   - - - - - - - - - - - - - - - - -
_____   _____
- - - - - - - - - - - - - - - - -   - - - - - - - - - - - - - - - - -
_____   _____
- - - - - - - - - - - - - - - - -   - - - - - - - - - - - - - - - - -
_____   _____
                                    - - - - - - - - - - - - - - - - -
                                    _____
                                    - - - - - - - - - - - - - - - - -
                                    _____
                                    - - - - - - - - - - - - - - - - -
                                    _____

Name ______________________________

I read

It was about

Words I Can Now Read and Write

© Pearson Education 1